STIR UP A S

Creative Writing Ideas

- Story Starters
- What If Stories
- Imagination Boosters
- Story Enders
- Short Stories

ants

Written by Linda Polon   **Illustrated by Beverly Armstrong**

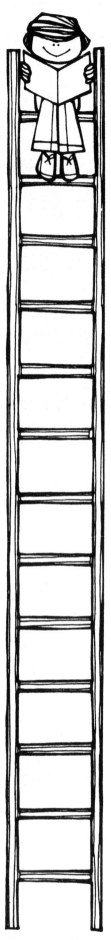

THE LEARNING WORKS
P.O. Box 6187 Santa Barbara, CA 93160

To The Teacher

Children like to write, but many don't like to be told to do it. The purpose of this book is to stir their imaginations so that they will write because they **want** to, not because they **have** to.

This book offers children a variety of writing experiences. Materials in the Story Starters, What If, Imagination Boosters, and Story Enders sections are self-motivating and can be used without additional explanation. Activities in the Short Story section may require some preliminary discussion. Even though each story type (for example, a fairy tale or mystery) is described and the method for writing it is explained, you may want to supplement this information with additional details or examples.

Help each child bind some of his or her stories and illustrations into a book. If possible, also create a class collection of stories. Ask each child to select his or her favorite story and illustration. By means of the thermofax or photocopy process, make enough copies of each story and picture so that you can bind a complete collection for each child as a gift at holiday time or as a special memento at the end of the year.

Copyright © 1981
THE LEARNING WORKS, INC.
P.O. Box 6187
Santa Barbara, CA 93160
All rights reserved.
Printed in the United States of America

CONTENTS

Name _____

THE SUBSTITUTE TEACHER

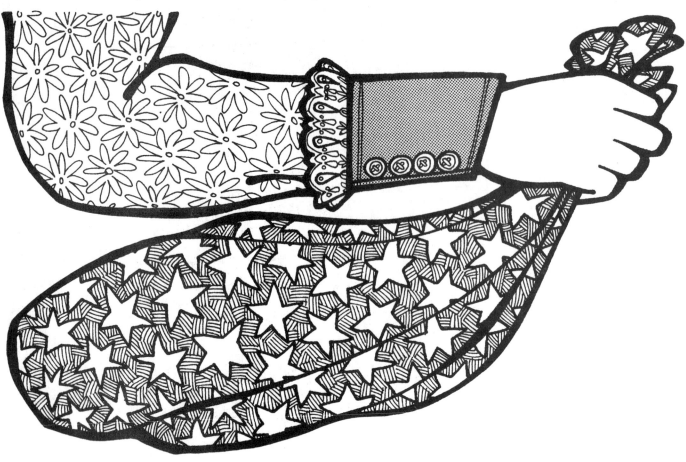

I couldn't believe what happened the day we had a substitute teacher! It all started when this lady walked into our classroom carrying a large, strange-looking sack and

_____

_____

_____

_____

_____

_____

_____

Name _____

WATCHING TELEVISION

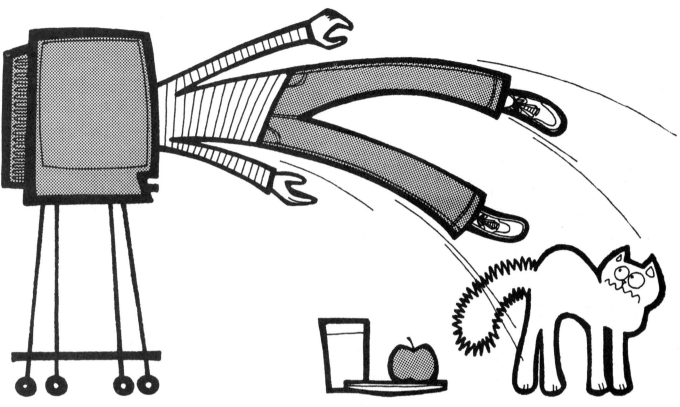

Something strange happened while I was watching television the other night. The TV set made a loud, crackling sound and a fuzzy glow appeared. I felt a tug. A second later, I was pulled inside the TV. Suddenly, I was in costume on the set of my favorite television program. The next thing I knew I was _____

_____

_____

_____

_____

_____

_____

_____

_____

Name _____

THE NIGHTMARE

I awoke in the middle of the night breathing hard. Sweat covered my forehead. My body trembled as I recalled the horrible dream in which I had barely escaped alive. It all started when _____

_____

_____

_____

_____

_____

_____

_____

Name _____

THE FOGGY MIST

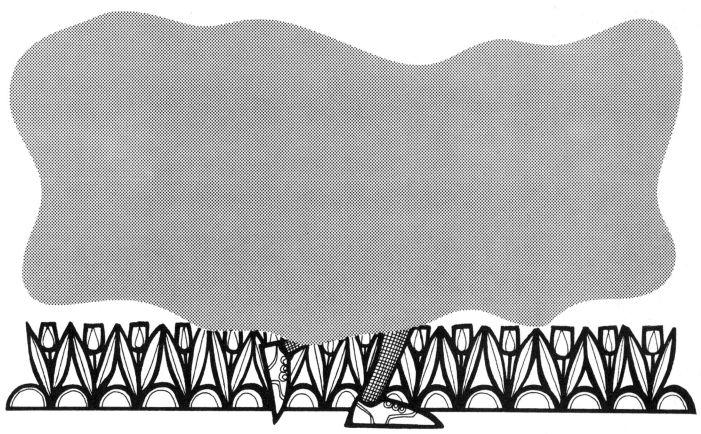

As I walked home from school, a foggy mist settled around me. A sudden chill crept through my body. In the next second, I felt my feet leave the ground. Before I knew it, I was _____

_____

_____

_____

_____

_____

_____

_____

Name _____

ABOARD THE SPACECRAFT

One dark, cloudy evening, a strange buzzing echoed from my backyard. Being a brave and curious person, I tiptoed outside. There in front of me was a silver spaceship with flashing red-and-green lights. Suddenly, a door slid open and a ladder extended down to the ground. Cautiously, I climbed the ladder and_____

_____

_____

_____

_____

_____

_____

_____

Name _____

VEGETABLES, VEGETABLES

   Over and over again, my parents told me to eat all of the vegetables on my plate or I wouldn't grow up big and strong. For weeks and weeks, I stuffed my face with lima beans, brussels sprouts, and carrots because I wanted to be tall and powerful. Then one day, the strangest thing happened. I _____

_____

_____

_____

_____

_____

_____

_____

9

Name _____

THE TROPHY

The trophy was large and had my name on it because I had broken a world's record. I had worked for months and months in preparation for the record-breaking event. It all started when I decided to _____

_____

_____

_____

_____

_____

_____

_____

_____

Name _____

MAGIC DUST

A yellow dust sprinkled down from fluffy clouds over our school yard. Before I knew it, everybody around me started laughing and couldn't stop. For some reason, I was the only one who wasn't laughing, so I _____

_____

_____

_____

_____

_____

_____

_____

_____

Name _____

FIRST PRIZE

What if you won first prize in a contest you entered? What type of contest would it be? Describe what you had to do to enter. Tell about your winning entry and your fabulous prize. What are you going to do with that prize?

_____

_____

_____

_____

_____

_____

_____

_____

Name _____

CHANGING PLACES

What if you were given the power to change places with any fairy tale character. Which one would it be and why? How would you act? Would you change your part in the fairy tale? Tell how you would change the beginning, middle, or the end of the story if you were in it.

_____

_____

_____

_____

_____

_____

_____

Name _____

YOUR MASTERPIECE

What if you were an artist and had created the most magnificent one-of-a-kind masterpiece the whole world had ever seen. Museums across the world wanted to display it. Describe your masterpiece and how you created it. Tell why it has become so popular.

_____

_____

_____

_____

_____

_____

_____

_____

Name _____

A NEW SPORT

Sports enthusiasts are crying for a new, competitive game. They have come to you for help. Can you create a game that will be as exciting as football, baseball, basketball, tennis, racquet ball, bowling, or soccer? Give your new game a name. Explain the rules and how it's played. Why will your new game be so popular?

_____

_____

_____

_____

_____

_____

_____

Name _____

TALKING PET

What if your pet or an animal you like started talking to you? What might the animal say? How would you feel? What would you say? Describe your conversation.

_____

_____

_____

_____

_____

_____

_____

Name _____

CHARACTER ALIVE

What if your favorite book character came to life for a day. Who would you want it to be? How would you spend the day together? Where would you go? What would you talk about?

_____

_____

_____

_____

_____

_____

_____

_____

Name _____

THE SHOPPING SPREE

What if you were given a free shopping spree in any department store. You could keep everything you picked out in ten minutes. To what store would you go? What things would you want and why? Describe your shopping spree.

_____

_____

_____

_____

_____

_____

_____

_____

Name _____

NO SCHOOL

What if there were no more school? How would you **really** feel? Where would you go during the day? How would you learn? How would you make friends? What would you do?

_____

_____

_____

_____

_____

_____

_____

Name _____

A NEW SCHOOL

What if you were given the chance to redesign your school? How would you make it different and more comfortable for kids? What would you change on the playground, in the cafeteria (don't forget the food, too), and in the classrooms?

_____

_____

_____

_____

_____

_____

_____

_____

Name _____

CAREER WEEK

For Career Week at school you are given the opportunity to take on an adult job in the community. What job would you choose and why? What special or different thing would you do in that position that isn't usually done? Describe your week at work.

_____

_____

_____

_____

_____

_____

_____

_____

_____

_____

_____

Name _____

DEAD SILENCE

Imagine a day that no one on earth could talk. It happened. How did it come about? How did people around the world **react** to it? Could the world get along without talking? If you couldn't speak, how would you communicate with your family and friends? What problems come from talking? What problems might come from **not** talking?

_____

_____

_____

_____

_____

_____

_____

_____

Name _____

RIGHT AND WRONG

Friends may not believe the two days you had. They were complete opposites. On one day, everything went right for you. On the other day, everything went wrong. Tell about your two days. What happened on each one? Why did these two days happen?

_____

_____

_____

_____

_____

_____

_____

_____

_____

_____

Name _____

IT'S FREE

For one day, everything in your city will be free. Nothing will cost money. Where will you go? What will you do? Why?

_____

_____

_____

_____

_____

_____

_____

_____

_____

_____

_____

APRIL FOOLS' DAY

For April Fools' Day you decided to play a safe but terrific joke on someone. Tell about your great joke and whom you would play it on. How would you make sure it would work? How would the person you are playing it on react?

_____

_____

_____

_____

_____

_____

_____

_____

_____

_____

Name _____

RAIN, RAIN, RAIN

It has rained for a week. In front of your house, the street is like a river. The electricity in your house is off. Only the candles burn at night. You can't go outdoors. How do you feel? What will you do to occupy your time? What hardships will you and your family endure?

_____

_____

_____

_____

_____

_____

_____

_____

26

Name _____

BUS TRIP

Your class has been given a bus trip. Each class member has been asked to tell where he or she would like to go, and the teacher will choose the best one. Tell what trip you'd like. Where would you go? Why would you go there? Why would your trip be fun? Because most school trips must be educational, explain what the kids would learn from your trip.

_____

_____

_____

_____

_____

_____

_____

_____

_____

Name _____

AROUND THE WORLD

You have won two around-the-world airplane tickets. You and a companion can travel by plane from your city around the world and back to your city with all expenses paid. What person will you take along and why? What special stuff will you take? What countries will you visit? Why? What souvenirs and other special things will you bring home from your travels? What exciting things would you like to have happen to you on your trip?

_____

_____

_____

_____

_____

_____

_____

_____

_____

Name _____

SAFE AT LAST

_____

_____

_____

_____

_____

_____

_____

_____

_____

_____

_____

_____

Finally, I tore out of the house and sped down the path leading to the street. I felt my heart pumping in my throat. I was out at last. I was safe.

Name _____

THE NIGHT THE NOISE STOPPED

_____

_____

_____

_____

_____

_____

_____

_____

_____

_____

_____

On a night when the moon was shining, the stars sparkling, and the sky a clear black, the noise finally stopped. Everybody in the small town of Cedar Hill sighed. It was all over at last.

Name _____

THE CONTEST

_____

_____

_____

_____

_____

_____

_____

_____

_____

_____

_____

    Everybody watched. The contest lasted for two hours. I was nervous the whole
time. The sweat rolled off my whole body, but I finally won.

31

Story Enders

Name _____

DESERVING TO WIN

_____
_____
_____
_____
_____
_____
_____
_____
_____
_____
_____

It took a long time to make. It almost got fouled up many times. The competition was rough, but I deserved to win.

Name _____

THE UNKNOWN HERO

_____

_____

_____

_____

_____

_____

_____

_____

_____

_____

_____

_____

"What a day," I thought as I fell back sleepily on my bed. "Nobody would have believed that I was a hero at school today, but I was."

Name _____

FEAR IS FOR OTHERS

_____

_____

_____

_____

_____

_____

_____

_____

_____

_____

I might have been frightened like the others, but I wasn't. Thank goodness I knew all along who did it!

Name _____

UNEASY EARNINGS

_____

_____

_____

_____

_____

_____

_____

_____

_____

_____

_____

    It was always easy earning my allowance until this week. What strange and funny things I had to do! I'm glad it's over now.

Name _____

FAIRY TALES

To bake a cake, you need to know what ingredients to use. To write a fairy tale, you need to know what ingredients make up that kind of story.

Fairy tales involve magic, love, and adventure. They are often about fairies who grant wishes, giants, handsome princes, beautiful princesses, and witches who cast spells. And they all begin with words like *Once upon a time* or *Long ago and far away* or *In old times when wishes still came true.*

The first part of a fairy tale is called the **introduction.** In this beginning part of the story, the characters (good and evil ones), the time and place of the story, the theme, and the problem or conflict are introduced. The **theme** is the basic idea of the story, or what the fairy tale is about. For example, "Jack and the Beanstalk" is about a poor widow who is forced by poverty to send her son, Jack, to town to sell their last remaining possession, a broken-down old cow.

After the introduction comes the body of the fairy tale, or **plot**. The plot is the heart of the story and the longest part of the tale. It begins where the introduction ends. In it the problem or conflict gets solved or resolved in one way or another. For example, Jack returns from town with a handful of beans. His mother is so upset about his having made such a stupid trade that she throws the beans out the window. Overnight, they grow into a magic beanstalk that reaches up through the clouds. At the top of the stalk is the castle of a wealthy giant. Jack and his mother live on the coins the boy is able to take from the giant's treasure chest. Temporarily, the problem of poverty is solved.

Toward the end of the plot, a **climax** is reached. The climax is the most interesting or exciting part of the story. In "Jack and the Beanstalk," the giant awakens to discover Jack raiding his treasure and chases him down the beanstalk. Seeing her son coming with the giant close behind, Jack's mother begins chopping down the beanstalk.

The last part of a fairy tale is called the **conclusion**. It is as short as the introduction. In it, the loose ends are tied up, and the story comes to an end. Slim Jack makes it safely to the ground, but the weakened stalk breaks under the weight of the giant. He crashes to the ground and is killed. With the coins Jack has gotten and without the evil giant to threaten them, Jack and his mother live happily ever after. Fairy tales always have a happy ending and often end with the words *They lived happily ever after.*

Now it's your turn to write a fairy tale. What will your tale be about? Think of the different ingredients before you begin writing. Will you include a tearful princess or a horrible dragon among the characters, or write about a magic potion or witch's spell? When you have finished writing, give your fairy tale a title and draw an illustration.

MYSTERY STORIES

What must a good mystery story have? It should be imaginative, entertaining, full of fast-moving action, and mysterious. It must create an atmosphere of excitement and suspense. **Suspense** is the air of uncertainty that runs through a mystery story. The reader should be kept wondering what is going to happen next. A mystery story should have a **puzzle** or **secret** that cannot easily be solved or discovered. It must involve a **character** or **characters** who can track down **clues** in spite of all obstacles or dangers to solve the mystery.

The plot of a mystery story must be finely crafted, step by step, building to a suspenseful **climax.** The climax comes near the end of the story when the mystery is about to be solved. The plot must be logical with realistic details and clues that will help a reader discover the mystery's solution. In other words, the plot must be supported by carefully chosen details and not have loose ends.

A mystery must have good **characterization**. Usually it is through one character that the mystery is solved. It is important that the writer make this character seem real to the reader. The writer must know the character and know why the character does what he or she does.

Another important part of a mystery is the **background** or **setting**. The setting is established at the beginning of the story, along with the character and the mystery. The setting can be an abandoned warehouse, an island, a city, or even a school. Dark or threatening settings add to the suspense and make the story even more mysterious. To make the story believable, the writer must be familiar with the setting.

Mysteries can center on anything. They can center on a strange, empty house on the top of a hill, a rusty key that opens a trunk, or a pie missing from a windowsill. They can be about sports, camping trips, a day spent shopping in the city, a birthday party, or a vacation.

Now it's your turn to write a mystery. Make sure you choose a good title, one that promises excitement or adventure. For example, you may wish to include the word *mystery* in your title or to call your story "The Case of the Mysterious . . . ." Consider such titles as

The Mysterious Stranger   The Strange Present   The Disappearing Friend
The Case of the Missing Homework   The Mystery of the Haunted House

Before you actually write the story, describe the mystery to be solved and the main characters. Then list the steps the character or characters will follow to solve the mystery, the clues that will be presented, and the obstacles the characters will encounter. To make others want to read your story, write an opening sentence that is interesting and promises intrigue and mystery. When you have finished writing, give your mystery a title and draw an illustration.

Name _____

HOW-TO STORIES

Can you write a story about how to roller skate backwards, make costumes, build a clubhouse out of odds and ends, or feed and care for a goldfish? Stories of this kind are called **how-to stories.**

Before you begin a how-to story, you must know your subject (what you are writing about). You may need to learn more about it by interviewing people or doing research in the library.

Once you know about your subject, make a list or outline of what you plan to include in your story. Then begin. Pretend that your readers know nothing about your topic. Write clear and easy-to-follow instructions so that they can understand, step by step, how to make or do the things you are explaining. Where possible, include drawings that show what is being made or the steps you are describing. Most important, don't let your story become boring. Make it fun to read.

Now it's your turn to write a how-to story. Use one of these titles

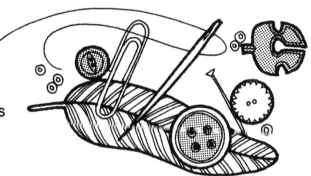

How to Collect Trading Cards

Safe Tricks on Skateboards

Cooking with Chocolate

How to Raise Parakeets

How to Make Puppets out of Socks

How to Play Kickball

or think up your own. To see if you wrote a good how-to story, ask someone who knows nothing about your subject to read it. If that person understands your instructions, your story is a success.

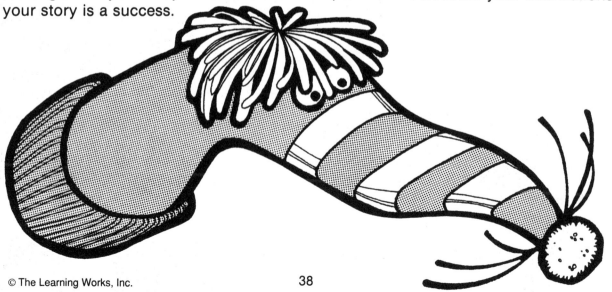

Name _____

TALL TALES

Tall tales are stories in which the truth or meaning is stretched or exaggerated for humorous effect. These stories were first told in America during the 1800s. To entertain one another, the pioneers made up stories in which they exaggerated the traits people had and the things they did.

The story of Paul Bunyan is an example of a tall tale. In this story, Paul weighs eighty pounds at birth, grows at the rate of two feet a day, and becomes so strong and tall that he can chop down an entire forest in two hours!

Tall tales are made up of exaggerated sentences. Stretch your imagination to complete each sentence below.

1. The man was so strong that _____

   _____

2. The girl could hear so well that _____

   _____

3. The boy was so thin that _____

   _____

4. The music was so loud that _____

   _____

5. It rained so hard all over town that _____

   _____

6. The lady was so smart that _____

   _____

7. The little child laughed so hard that _____

   _____

8. The machine worked so hard that _____

   _____

The girl could hear so well that she could hear a butterfly breathing. HUFF PUFF

Name _____

TALL TALES

Now it's your turn to write a tall tale. Use one of these titles

    The Funniest Person in the World

    The Man Who Wouldn't Stop Talking

    The Strongest Person in the World

    The River That Flowed on Forever and Ever

or think up your own. Use the outline below to help you write your exaggerated story. Describe the main parts of your story by filling in the blanks *before* you start to write.

Main Character List physical strengths and weaknesses and qualities of appearance, such as height, size, and color of hair and eyes.

1. _____

2. _____

3. _____

4. _____

5. _____

Setting Describe where the story takes place.

_____

_____

_____

_____

Plot Describe what happens to the main character and what he or she does in the story.

_____

_____

_____

_____

Write your story on a separate piece of paper. Don't forget to give it a title and draw at least one illustration.

FABLES

A long time ago, a storyteller name Aesop wrote fables. **Fables** are short stories in which human weaknesses or faults are described mostly through the words and actions of animals. Aesop's stories were designed to teach a lesson, and at the end of each, he wrote what the lesson, or **moral**, was.

An example of a fable is "The Boy Who Cried Wolf." This fable is about a boy who takes care of sheep in the fields outside a small town. Because he grows bored and lonely by himself in the field, he frequently cries, "Wolf!" At his cry of alarm, men and women from the town rush out to the fields to help him. Of course, after several "false alarms," they realize that the boy is fooling them. When a wolf really does attack and the boy once again calls for help, the townsfolk ignore his cries. Nobody comes to his rescue.

The moral to the story is that if you complain and cry for help when you don't need it, no one will believe you when you really do.

Now it's your turn to write a fable. Use some of these characters

      a snake and a gorilla

      a koala and a kangaroo

      a monkey and an ant

      a sea otter, a walrus, and a starfish

or think up some of your very own. Don't forget to have your story teach a lesson. State the lesson, or moral, at the end. Write your fable on a separate piece of paper. Draw at least one illustration.

      41

Name _____

BIOGRAPHIES

The dictionary states that a **biography** is an account of one person's life written or told by another person.

Biographies are written about women and men, living or dead, who did not give up in the face of danger or unfavorable odds and were, therefore, able to accomplish something unusual or special. They are people who had the courage and determination to follow their dreams and put their beliefs into practice. For example, Martin Luther King, Jr., a religious leader, fought for equal rights for all. Ludwig van Beethoven, a composer, went deaf but continued to write beautiful music. And Marie Curie, a scientist, discovered the chemical element radium.

Biographies are written about astronauts, explorers, heroes and heroines, historical figures, inventors, and presidents. Today, some biographies focus on the accomplishments of men and women who have become famous in the sports world or in the motion picture or television industry.

Before you write a biography, select a person to write about. Choose someone you like and can identify with or someone you don't know but want to learn more about. Next, get to know the person you have chosen. Where was this person born? Where did this person live? How was this person prepared in early life for later accomplishments? What traits or characteristics made this person different?

Now it's your turn to write a biography. Make your subject come alive for your readers. Don't forget to draw a picture.

John Muir,
Earth-planet,
Universe

Name _____

AUTOBIOGRAPHIES

An **autobiography** is a story its author writes about his or her own life. Your autobiography is your account of your life from the day you were born until now. What information should you include in a story about yourself? How do you remember everything about yourself and the experiences you had as you were growing up? It would be a good idea to search your memory and write down the events you remember. Next, interview your parents and relatives and ask them questions like these:

1. Where and when was I born? _____

_____

2. Was I a good baby or did I cry a lot? _____

_____

3. What was my favorite toy? _____

_____

4. What things did I like to do? _____

_____

_____

5. Did I get into much mischief? _____

_____

6. At what age did I learn to walk? _____

7. At what age did I learn to talk? _____

8. What funny things did I say? _____

_____

9. What trips did I take? _____

_____

_____

10. Did I like school at first? _____

_____

11. Did I usually get along well with my brothers and sisters? _____

_____

What other question might you ask?

    Once you have discovered enough facts about yourself, write your autobiography on a separate piece of paper. Remember that you do not have to tell everything that ever happened to you. Choose the events that are the most unusual or are the most exciting or the most fun to recall. Chances are these are the ones your reader will find most interesting.

43

Name _____

JUST SO STORIES

Just so stories were first written by an English writer named Rudyard Kipling. In them he described, among other things, "How the Whale Got His Spout" and "How the Leopard Got His Spots." In his just so stories, Kipling supplied unusual or imaginative explanations for obvious or observable natural conditions or situations.

Now it's your turn to write a just so story. Choose one of the following topics

How the Raccoon Got a Black Mask

How the Bee Got Its Stinger

How the Octopus Got So Many Legs

How the Peanut Got in the Shell

How the Roadrunner Got Started Running

How the Strawberry Got Its Red Color

or think up one of your own. Don't forget to give your story a just so title and to include an illustration or two.

Name _____

ANIMAL STORIES

Animal Stories are stories written primarily about animals. There may be some people in the stories, but the main characters are animals.

There are several types of animal stories: fantastic, realistic, and scientific. An **animal fantasy** is an animal story in which the animals talk and experience emotions like people and may even wear clothes. This type of story deals with many of the same plot ideas (conflicts and problems) found in stories about people. The animals may be finding a home, having a party, playing a baseball game, or going on a diet. A. A. Milne's *The House at Pooh Corner,* E.B. White's *Charlotte's Web,* and Michael Bond's *A Bear Called Paddington* are good examples of animal fantasy.

Even though an animal fantasy is a make-believe story, the setting and plot must seem believable to the reader. As you write, keep in mind the places in which particular animals are found and how the natural characteristics of animals might determine the way they would talk or act and what they would be able to do. For example, because of the way their hind legs are constructed, kangaroos are very good at bounding and leaping, but elephants cannot jump at all.

Some animals stories are **realistic.** Like animal fantasy, these stories are fiction (made up, not true), but they are true to life. In these stories, the animals don't talk. They make normal animal sounds and perform in usual ways, but they play a central role in a series of fast-moving adventures and narrow escapes. *Black Beauty* by Anna Sewell and *The Black Stallion* by Walter Farley are realistic animal stories.

Other animal stories are **scientific.** They are nonfiction and recount the actual observations and experiences of people who have worked closely with animals. Joy Adamson's book *Born Free* is a scientific animal story about a lioness named Elsa.

Now it's your turn to write an animal story. Choose one of the types described above. When you have finished your animal story, illustrate it.

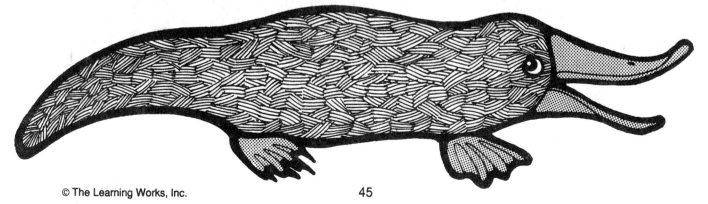

Name _____

SCIENCE FICTION STORIES

Science fiction is fiction written about the effects of real or imagined science on the people and societies of the future. It often pits people against the machines and monsters of other worlds and usually has elements of danger and adventure. The setting is sometimes outer space. The story may involve other planets and their life forms or visitations by these life forms to earth.

In a science fiction story, the equipment, gadgets, clothing, furniture, and food are all different from what we now know on earth. Even though these objects may never exist and the plot may never come true, the writer must describe and explain them in ways that make them believable to the reader. *Star Wars* and *The Empire Strikes Back* are examples of science fiction, as are *Journey to the Center of the Earth* by Jules Verne and *The Time Machine* by H.G. Wells.

Now it's your turn to write a science fiction story. Use one of these titles

The Journey to Planet Mysterious

The Computer War

Space Shuttle Breakdown

The Night Visitors

Future Calling

or think up your own. When you have finished writing your story, illustrate it.

Name _____

ADVENTURE STORIES

An **adventure story** is a story about a dangerous or risky undertaking. In it the main characters face a variety of dangers and challenges to achieve a goal. Because it involves the unknown and the outcome is uncertain, it is exciting and suspenseful. It may take place in the mountains, on the ocean, on the desert, in the air, or in a foreign country.

In an adventure story, the main character or characters are involved in daring exploits and challenging situations. The plot is fast-paced and keeps them on the go. They hunt for gold, dive for sunken treasure, chase a man-eating shark, cross the ocean on a raft, climb the world's highest mountain, sail around the world, or fly across the United States beneath a hot air balloon. *The Call of the Wild* by Jack London and *The Incredible Journey* by Sheila Burnford are examples of adventure stories.

Now it's your turn to write an adventure story. Use one of these titles

The Runaway Train

The Great Trip

The Treasure Hunt

The Snow Journey

The Adventure of Three Friends

or think up one of our own. Write your story on a separate piece of paper. When you have finished writing your story, illustrate it.

Name _____

SPORTS STORIES

A **sports story** is a story that has a sports theme. The story revolves around a sport like baseball, basketball, football, kickball, swimming, soccer, or tetherball. It can be about a single superstar or an entire team. Most of the action takes place when the sport is being talked about, planned for, and played by the main **characters**.

A sports story can be humorous, adventurous, or mysterious. A humorous sports story may involve members of a boys' baseball team who discover that their best player is a girl in disguise. A mysterious sports story could be about the strange disappearance of sports equipment from the locker room **before each game**. An adventurous sports story could take a team to different countries like China to play their games.

Now it's your turn to write a sports story. First, choose a sport. You will probably find it easier to write about a sport with which you are familiar. Next, select a location. Then, decide how your main character or characters are involved in the sport, what conflicts confront them, and what problems they must solve. **To help you write your** story, use one of these titles

The Missing Equipment

Three More to Go

The Long Race

The Strange Win

The Struggle

The Triumph

or think up your own. Write and illustrate your story on a **separate piece of paper.**

RANDY AND HIS REMOTE CONTROL TETHERBALL